Where Are We Going?

Christine Finochio • Jennette MacKenzie

"We are going away,"
said Mom. "We are going
on a trip."

3

"Where are we going?" asked Brian.

"Are we going to the beach?" asked Sandra.

"Are we going camping?" asked Brian.

"How long will we be away?" asked Sandra.

"It's a surprise," said Mom. "Pack your bags. Pack your pants and shirts. Pack your socks and shoes."

"Pack your toothbrush and comb. Pack your teddy bear and your blanket," said Mom.

9

"Pack your jacket and your book. But don't pack the cats!" said Dad.

"Oh, Dad!" said Sandra and Brian.

"Where are we going? Please tell us!"

"It's a surprise!" said Dad.

"Put your bags in the car."

"What about the cats?"

asked Sandra.

"Grandpa is going to look

after the cats," said Dad.

"Are we going by plane?" asked Brian.

"We are going for a trip on the train," said Mom.

"Hooray!" shouted Brian.

"We are going to visit Uncle Bob and Aunt Kate," said Mom.

"We are going to see their new baby."